Seitan Cookbook

Easy Protein Packed Vegan Meat Recipes for Beginners from BBQ, Stir Fry to Tacos and More

Jenny Kern

Table Of Contents

Introduction

Thank you very much for purchasing this cookbook. Seitan has a long history. It is a traditional food in China, Korea, and Japan, where it was originally prepared by vegetarian Buddhist monks, and has long been used frequently in the United States, Mormons, and Seventh-day Adventists. It comes from gluten, the protein part of wheat, which is mixed with water and then cooked with spices and flavorings.

The word seitan was coined in the 1960s by macrobiotics expert George Ohsawa. Sei means "is" while the term tan comes from the term tanpaku, "protein". Hence, seitan, correctly translated, means something like the right protein substitute. The Chinese call wheat gluten mien chin or yu mien ching. Chinese restaurants often refer to wheat gluten as "Buddha Food," a definition that echoes its origin. I hope my recipes can satisfy your palate.

Enjoy your meal.

Breakfast Recipes

1. Seitan Meatza with Kale

Preparation Time: 10 Minutes

Cooking Time: 22 Minutes

Servings: 4

Ingredients:

1 lb. ground seitan

1 tsp Salt and black pepper to taste

2 cups powdered Parmesan cheese

¼ tsp onion powder

¼ tsp garlic powder

½ cup unsweetened tomato sauce

1 tsp white vinegar

½ tsp liquid smoke

¼ cup baby kale, chopped roughly

1 cup mozzarella cheese

Directions:

1. Preheat the oven to 400°F and line a medium pizza pan with parchment paper and grease with cooking spray. Set aside.

2. In a medium bowl, combine the seitan, salt, black pepper, and parmesan cheese. Spread the mixture on the pizza pan to fit the shape of the pan. Bake in the oven for 15 minutes or until the meat cooks.
3. Meanwhile in a medium bowl, mix the onion powder, garlic powder, tomato sauce, vinegar, and liquid smoke. Remove the meat crust from the oven and spread the tomato mixture on top. Add the kale and sprinkle with the mozzarella cheese.
4. Bake in the oven for 7 minutes or until the cheese melts. Take out from the oven, slice, and serve warm.

2. Seitan & Spinach Salad a la Puttanesca

Preparation Time: 10 Minutes

Cooking Time: 20 Minutes

Servings: 4

Ingredients:

4 tbsp olive oil

8 oz seitan, cut into strips

2 garlic cloves, minced

½ cup Kalamata olives, halved

½ cup green olives, halved

2 tbsp capers

3 cups baby spinach, cut into strips

1 ½ cups cherry tomatoes, halved

2 tbsp balsamic vinegar

2 tbsp torn fresh basil leaves

2 tbsp minced fresh parsley

1 cup pomegranate seeds

Directions:

1. Heat half of the olive oil in a skillet over medium heat. Place the seitan and brown for 5 minutes on all sides.
2. Add in garlic and cook for 30 seconds. Remove to a bowl and let cool.
3. Stir in olives, capers, spinach, and tomatoes. Set aside.
4. In another bowl, whisk the remaining oil, vinegar, salt, and pepper until well mixed.
5. Pour this dressing over the seitan salad and toss to coat.
6. Top with basil, parsley, and pomegranate seeds. Serve.

3. Black Forest Bread

Preparation Time: 2 hours 15 minutes

Cooking Time: 50 minutes

Servings: 1 loaf

Ingredients:

1 ⅛ cups warm water

⅓ cup Molasses

1 ½ tbsp Canola oil

1 ½ cups bread flour

1 cup Rye flour

1 cup Whole wheat flour

1 ½ tsp salt

Three tbsp Cocoa powder

1 ½ tbsp Caraway seeds

Two tsp Active dry yeast

Directions:

1. Place all ingredients into your bread maker according to manufacture.
2. Select type to a light crust, then press start.
3. If the mixture is too dry, add a tbsp of warm water at a time.
4. If the mixture is too wet, add flour again a little at a time.
5. The mixture should go into a ball form, and just soft and slightly sticky to the finger touch. It goes for all types of bread when kneading.

4. Molasses Wheat Bread

Preparation Time: 10 minutes or less

Cooking Time: 1 hour 30 minutes

Servings: 10

Ingredients:

8 slices / 1 lb.

½ cup water, at 80°F to 90°F

¼ cup milk, at 80°F

2 tsp melted butter, cooled

2 tbsp honey

1 tbsp molasses

1 tsp sugar

1 tbsp skim milk powder

½ tsp salt

1 tsp unsweetened cocoa powder

1¼ cups whole-wheat flour

1 cup white bread flour

1 tsp bread machine yeast or instant yeast

12 slices / 1½ pounds

¾ cup water, at 80°F to 90°F

⅓ cup milk, at 80°F

1 tbsp melted butter, cooled

3¾ tbsp honey

2 tbsp molasses

2 tsp sugar

2 tbsp skim milk powder

¾ tsp salt

2 tsp unsweetened cocoa powder

1¾ cups whole-wheat flour

1¼ cups white bread flour

1⅛ tsp bread machine yeast or instant yeast

16 slices / 2 pounds

1 cup water, at 80°F to 90°F

½ cup milk, at 80°F

2 tbsp melted butter, cooled

5 tbsp honey

3 tbsp molasses

1 tbsp sugar

3 tbsp skim milk powder

1 tsp salt

1 tbsp unsweetened cocoa powder

2½ cups whole-wheat flour

2 cups white bread flour

1½ tsp bread machine or instant yeast

Directions:

1. Place the ingredients in your bread machine as recommended by the manufacturer.
2. Program the machine for Basic/White bread, select light or medium crust, and press Start.
3. When the loaf is done, remove the bucket from the machine.
4. Let the loaf cool for 5 minutes.
5. Gently shake the bucket to remove the loaf and turn it out onto a rack to cool.

Ingredient tip: Look for unsulfured molasses because it is sweeter and lacks the slight chemical taste of sulfured products. Also, this bread is best with sticky, rich dark or blackstrap molasses instead of light-colored molasses.

5. Cornmeal Whole Wheat Bread

Preparation Time: 1 hour and 30 minutes

Cooking Time: 30 minutes

Servings: 10

Ingredients:

Active dry yeast – 2 ½ tsps.

Water – 1 ⅓ cups.

Sugar – 2 tbsp.

Egg – 1, lightly beaten

Butter – 2 tbsp.

Salt – 1 ½ tsps.

Cornmeal – ¾ cup.

Whole wheat flour – ¾ cup.

Bread flour – 2 ¾ cups.

Directions:

1. Add all ingredients to the bread machine pan according to the bread machine manufacturer's instructions.
2. Select basic bread setting then select medium crust and start.
3. Once the loaf is done, remove the loaf pan from the machine.
4. Allow it to cool for 10 minutes. Slice and serve.

6. Basic White Bread

Preparation time: 5 minutes

Cooking time: 3 hours

Servings: 16

Ingredients:

1 cup warm water (about 110°F/45°C)

2 Tbsp sugar

2¼ tsp (.25-ounce package) bread machine yeast

¼ cup rice bran oil

3 cups bread flour

1 tsp salt

Directions:

1. Add each ingredient to the bread machine in the order and at the temperature recommended by your bread machine manufacturer.
2. Close the lid, select the basic or white bread, low crust setting on your bread machine, and press start.
3. When the bread machine has finished baking, remove the bread and put it on a cooling rack.

7. Extra Buttery White Bread

Preparation time: 10 minutes

Cooking time: 3 hours 10 minutes

Servings: 16

Ingredients:

1 ⅛ cups milk

4 Tbsp unsalted butter

3 cups bread flour

1½ Tbsp white granulated sugar

1½ tsp salt

1½ tsp bread machine yeast

Directions:

1. Soften the butter in your microwave.
2. Add each ingredient to the bread machine in the order and at the temperature recommended by your bread machine manufacturer.
3. Close the lid, select the basic or white bread, medium crust setting on your bread machine, and press start.
4. When the bread machine has finished baking, remove the bread, and put it on a cooling rack.

8. Italian White Bread

Preparation time: 5 minutes

Cooking time: 3 hours

Servings: 14

Ingredients:

¾ cup cold water

2 cups bread flour

1 Tbsp sugar

1 tsp salt

1 Tbsp olive oil

1 tsp active dry yeast

Directions:

1. Add each ingredient to the bread machine in the order and at the temperature recommended by your bread machine manufacturer.
2. Close the lid, select the Italian or basic bread, low crust setting on your bread machine, and press start.
3. When the bread machine has finished baking, remove the bread and put it on a cooling rack.

Nibbles and Bites Recipes

9. Homemade Flour Tortillas

Preparation Time: 10 Minutes

Cooking Time: 30 Minutes

Servings: 4

Ingredients:

3 cups all-purpose white flour

1-2 tsp baking powder (optional)

¼ cup vegetable oil

¾ cup cold water

1 tsp salt

Extra flour, for dusting while rolling and cooking

Directions:

1. Combine the flour, baking powder, oil, and water in a bowl and knead lightly to make a dough. The dough should be soft and not sticky. Add a little more flour (if too gooey or sticky) or oil (if too stiff) to adjust the consistency.
2. Form into 20 or more balls and sprinkle with flour to keep them from drying out. Let them rest for 5-15 minutes and cover with a kitchen towel, depending on how much the dough was kneaded.
3. Use a rolling pin to flatten and shape the dough into discs of the desired thickness and diameter. Dust with flour to prevent sticking.
4. Using a nonstick pan, cook the freshly rolled-out tortillas one at a time (about 30 seconds on each side).
5. Cover the cooked tortillas with a clean kitchen towel to keep them soft and pliable.
6. Allow the cooked tortillas to cool under the towel. Cooled tortillas may be kept in resealable bags and frozen for later use. These can be kept frozen for several months but will not taste as good as freshly made tortillas.
7. To heat the tortillas, steam them by wrapping them in damp towels, 5 pieces at a time, and heating them in the microwave for 20-30 seconds. You may also heat them on a warm skillet for 15 seconds on each side.
8. May be served warm or cold.

10. Tequila-Lime Chicken Tacos

Preparation Time: 10 Minutes

Cooking Time: 30 Minutes

Servings: 4

Ingredients:

½ cup tequila

¼ cup lime juice

2 cloves garlic, minced

2 jalapeños, trimmed and minced

Salt and black pepper, to taste

1 lb. chicken breasts, skinless and chopped

1 tbsp canola oil

1 cup red cabbage, shredded

½ cup cottage cheese

1 cup fresh cilantro, for garnish

3 lime wedges, for a side serving

8 (6-inch) wheat tortillas, warm

Directions:

1. In a large baking dish, combine tequila, salt, pepper, garlic, and lime juice. Add the chicken to the baking dish and let it sit for 30 minutes to marinate. Add the oil to a large grill pan.
2. Let the chicken cook for 6 minutes per side on the grill. Layer the tacos with cooked chicken, cabbage, cilantro, jalapeños, and cottage cheese.
3. Serve with lime wedges.

11.Rancher's Breaded Chicken Tacos

Preparation Time: 10 Minutes

Cooking Time: 30 Minutes

Servings: 4

Ingredients:

2 pounds chicken, skinless and boneless, cut into 2-inch strips

1 ½ cups all-purpose flour

1 ½ cups panko breadcrumbs

2 large eggs, beaten

Salt and black pepper, to taste

1 cup barbecue sauce

½ cup brown sugar

2 tbsp lime juice

1 tsp garlic powder

12 (6-inch) flour tortillas

2 cups finely shredded lettuce such as Iceberg or Romaine

1 cup ranch dressing, for drizzling

½ cup fresh cilantro, for garnish

Directions:

1. Combine chicken and flour in a Ziploc bag. Shake well to coat. Preheat the oven to 450°F.
2. Take a large bowl and add panko breadcrumbs. In a separate bowl, whisk the eggs.
3. Dip the chicken in the eggs and then in the breadcrumbs to coat.
4. Transfer it to a parchment paper-lined baking dish. Sprinkle salt and pepper on top.
5. Bake chicken for 20 minutes. Meanwhile, heat a saucepan over low heat.
6. Add garlic powder, warm barbecue sauce, brown sugar, and lime juice to the saucepan. Coat the baked chicken with the glaze.
7. Prepare the tacos by placing the glazed chicken on top of the tortillas and finishing with a generous amount of lettuce and ranch dressing. Top with fresh cilantro.

12. Cheesy Chicken Tacos

Preparation Time: 10 Minutes

Cooking Time: 30 Minutes

Servings: 4

Ingredients:

1 tbsp olive oil

2 small yellow onions, chopped

1 tsp cumin

Salt and black pepper, to taste

2 cups shredded chicken, boneless

⅓ cup green chilies, or to taste

1 cup salsa

1 cup canned refried beans, rinsed and drained

10–12 hard taco shells

2 cups Pepper Jack cheese, shredded

Directions:

1. Preheat the oven to 375°F. Heat the oil in a skillet over medium heat.
2. Add onions to the skillet and cook for 5 minutes. Add cumin, salt, and pepper.
3. Stir well and add chicken, green chilies, and salsa. Stir to combine ingredients well.
4. Layer half of the refried beans on a baking dish. Spoon the remaining beans into the taco shells and top each shell with the chicken mixture.
5. Place them on the baking dish so that they are standing up. Top the tacos with cheese and bake for 15 minutes.

13. Spongy Tamales Filled with Chile Strips and Cheese

Preparation Time: 10 Minutes

Cooking Time: 30 Minutes

Servings: 4

Ingredients:

For the Masa:

1 lb. (450 g) tamale flour

36 (to be safe) corn husks, soaked to tenderize and shaken dry

8 ounces (225 g) pork lard (approximately 1 cup/250 ml)

About 1 cup (250 ml) warm chicken broth

Salt to taste

For the Filling:

12 ounces (340 g) chihuahua, Mexican manchego, or muenster cheese, cut into strips about ½ inch (1.5 cm) wide

2 cups (500 ml) rajas of poblano chiles, approximately eight chiles

2 cups (500 ml) salsa de tomate verde

Directions:

1. Using an electric mixer, beat the lard until light and fluffy—about five minutes. Slowly beat in the flour alternately with the broth, beating meticulously after each addition. Put in salt. If beaten adequately, a small piece of dough should float on the surface of a glass of water.
2. Place a prepared tamale steamer using low heat.
3. Spread 1 heaped tbsp of the masa finely over the upper part, and about 3 inches (8 cm) down the leaf. Put 2 strips of the chile, a strip of the cheese, and a tbsp of the sauce over them.
4. Fold the husk so that the filling is mostly covered by the masa and turn the spare part of the husk up the back of the tamale.
5. Set the tamales vertically in the top part of the steamer, cover well, and steam for approximately 1¼ hours. To test, open up a tamale; the masa should separate cleanly from the husk.
6. Leave the tamales in the steamer until they are cool; they will become slightly firmer and less likely to break as you serve them.

14. Sweet Fresh Corn Tamales

Cooking Time: 30 Minutes

Servings: 4

Ingredients:

¼ tsp salt

½ tsp baking powder

1 cup (250 ml) grated piloncillo or dark brown sugar

1 small tbsp anise seeds

30 (to be safe) fresh corn husks, washed and shaken dry

4 cups (1 l) field or white starchy corn kernels

4 ounces (115 g) pork lard (½ cup/125 ml), melted and cooled

4 ounces (115 g) unsalted butter (½ cup/125 ml), melted and cooled

8-inch (20-cm) piece of cinnamon stick

About ½ cup (125 ml) water

Directions:

1. Ready a tamale steamer and line the top part with fresh corn husks.

2. Use a food processor/blender to blend the corn with the water, in two batches, to a rough-textured consistency—you will have to keep stopping the machine and loosening the mixture using a spatula, but do not put in more liquid.
3. Grind the spices into a powder and put them in with the sugar and salt to the corn, mixing meticulously.
4. Slowly mix in the fats and lastly the baking powder. Again, mix meticulously. The consistency must be that of a loose, textured paste.
5. Put approximately 1½ tbsp of the corn mixture down the center of each husk to extend about 3 inches (8 cm) long. Curl one side of the leaf over the mixture, ensuring there is a good overlap, and the mixture cannot ooze out.
6. Push the leaf tightly where the mixture ends and fold the empty part, and pointed end, to the back of the tamale.
7. Ensure that the water is boiling in the steamer, then lay the tamales in horizontal layers on the top of the steamer. It is best to put one layer in first and allow it to firm up a little—about ten minutes—before stacking the other layers on top.
8. Steam for approximately 1½ hours until, when tested, the dough separates cleanly from the husk.
9. Eat accompanied by a cup of atole or hot chocolate. Reheat this type of tamale, with the husk removed, on a comal or griddle on moderate heat.

15. Honey Chipotle Tacos

Preparation Time: 10 Minutes

Cooking Time: 30 Minutes

Servings: 4

Ingredients:

4 chicken breasts, cut into cubes

4 chipotle peppers, chopped

¼ cup adobo sauce

¼ cup honey

½ cup olive oil

1 tsp garlic powder

¼ tsp chili powder

Salt, to taste

1 tbsp vegetable oil

1 lime, sliced

12 hard taco shells

1 cup sour cream, for serving

Directions:

1. In a large bowl, combine pepper, adobo sauce, olive oil, honey, and all the spices. Mix well and then add chicken.
2. Mix to coat the chicken well. Cover the chicken with plastic wrap and refrigerate for 20 minutes.
3. Heat the vegetable oil in a skillet and cook the marinated chicken for 20 minutes. Assemble the tacos by layering the shells with cooked chicken, sour cream, and lime juice.

Lunch Recipes

16. Barbecue Baked Seitan Strips

Preparation Time: 10 Minutes

Cooking Time: 30 Minutes

Servings: 4

Ingredients:

½ cup nutritional yeast

3 cups vital wheat gluten

1 ½ tsp smoked paprika

1 ½ tbsp garlic powder

1 tsp onion powder

½ tsp dried oregano

½ tsp dried basil

3 ½ cups vegetable broth

2 cups vegan barbecue sauce

5 tbsp olive oil

5 tbsp maple syrup

3 tbsp soy sauce

1 tsp liquid smoke

1 tsp garlic powder

1 ½ tsp black pepper

Directions:

1. Preheat the oven to 390F. Mix gluten, yeast, 1 ½ tbsp garlic powder, 1 tsp smoked paprika, 1 tsp onion powder, ½ tsp black pepper, ½ tsp oregano, and ½ tsp basil in a bowl.
2. Mix 1 cup BBQ sauce, 2 tbsp maple syrup, 1 ½ cups vegetable broth, 2 tbsp olive oil, and 1 tbsp soy sauce in a bowl. Add liquid to dry ingredients and mix well. Knead the mixture until the dough is formed. Let rest.
3. Mix the remaining broth, BBQ sauce, maple syrup, olive oil, soy sauce, liquid smoke, black pepper, garlic powder, and smoked paprika in a bowl and mix well to make a marinade.
4. Place dough on a flat surface and flatten. Add a little oil and roll out to 1" thick and rectangle shape. Add 1 cup marinade to a tray and place dough on top. Cover with the remaining marinade. Bake for 1 hour adds 1 cup broth if it dries in between. Serve and enjoy.

17. Mongolian Seitan (Vegan Mongolian Beef)

Preparation Time: 10 Minutes

Cooking Time: 30 Minutes

Servings: 4

Ingredients:

2 tbsp + 2 tsp vegetable oil

3 garlic cloves, minced

½ tsp ginger, minced

⅓ tsp red pepper flakes

½ cup soy sauce

2 tsp corn starch

2 tbsp cold water

½ cup + 2 tbsp coconut sugar

1 lb. homemade seitan Rice, cooked

Directions:

1. Heat 2 tsp of vegetable oil in a pan over medium heat. Add garlic and ginger and mix well. Add red pepper flakes after 30 seconds and cook for 1 minute.

2. Add coconut sugar and soy sauce and mix well. Reduce the heat to medium-low and cook for 7 minutes. Mix cornstarch and water and add to the pan and mix well to combine. Cook for 3 minutes reduces the heat to the lowest and simmer.
3. Heat the remaining oil in a skillet over medium-high heat. Add the seitan and cook for 5 minutes.
4. Reduce the heat and add the sauce to the pan. Mix well to coat every seitan piece and cook until all sauce adheres. Remove from heat. Serve with rice.

18. Harissa Seitan and Green Beans

Preparation Time: 10 Minutes

Cooking Time: 30 Minutes

Servings: 4

Ingredients:

1 tbsp (15 ml) high heat neutral-flavored oil

8 ounces (227 g) Quit-the-Cluck Seitan, cut into ½-inch (1.3 cm) strips

2 handfuls green beans, trimmed, cut into bite-size pieces

½ of red bell pepper, cut into thin strips

1 leek, white part only, cut in half, sliced into half-rounds

½ cup (80 ml) dry red wine, or vegetable broth

1½ tbsp (24 g) harissa paste, or to taste

3 tbsp (48 g) tomato paste

1 cup (235 ml) vegetable broth

2 cloves garlic, minced Juice from ½ lemon

Salt and pepper

Directions:

1. Heat the oil in a large skillet over medium-high heat. Bake for 4 to 6 minutes, occasionally stirring to brown.
2. Add the green beans and cook for 3 minutes until they are green. Add the pepper and the leek and cook for 2 minutes, stirring to soften but not soft. Add a glass of wine (75 ml) of wine or broth to the pan and lower each bit. Reduce heat to medium. Add harissa paste, tomato paste, broth, garlic, and lemon juice. Stir to cover the olives and vegetables.
3. Cook for 10 minutes, stirring occasionally. Season with salt and pepper.

19. Seitan Fish

Preparation Time: 10 Minutes

Cooking Time: 30 Minutes

Servings: 4

Ingredients:

2 ½ cups Vital Wheat Gluten

1 to 2 tbsp Nori powder

6 cups Water

3 tbsp Seaweed Flakes, dried

2 tbsp Lemon juice

4 pieces Chinese mushroom, dried

1 ½ tsp Salt

1 tsp dried Garlic

Directions:

1. In a medium bowl, mix gluten powder, nori powder, and 2 cups of water until they form into dough. Knead the dough using your hands for about 10 minutes.
2. Shape the dough into thin fillets if you would like to make fish fillets. In a small pot, place the remaining water, together with seaweed, mushrooms, garlic, salt, and lemon juice.
3. Bring the broth to a slow boil. Drop the mock fish into the broth and let them simmer for at least 30 minutes.
4. After boiling, refrigerate overnight in the broth for a more seafood flavor. Your mock fish is now ready to use for any seafood recipe you have in mind.

20. Seitan Ham

Preparation Time: 10 Minutes

Cooking Time: 30 Minutes

Servings: 4

Ingredients:

1 ¾ cups Water

¼ cup Olive Oil

¼ cup Soy Sauce

¼ cup Nutritional Yeast

1 tsp Smoked Paprika

2 tsp Onion powder

1 tsp Garlic powder

1 tbsp Salt

2 tbsp Hickory Liquid Smoke

1 tbsp Maple Syrup (alternatively, you can use Brown Sugar or Molasses) ½ tsp Red Food Coloring

3 ¼ cups Vital Wheat Gluten

Directions:

1. Prepare the water steamer. In a bowl of a food processor, place all ingredients except the gluten flour and pulse until smooth.
2. Transfer in a mixing bowl and add the gluten flour, mixing until you have come up with the dough. Using your hands, knead the dough for a few minutes.
3. Cut the dough into 2 equal pieces and roll until it is shaped like a log. Wrap in a foil and twist both ends to seal.
4. Steam for about an hour. Preheat oven to 350°F.
5. Remove the seitan ham from the steamer and place it in a baking tray. Bake for 40 to 50 minutes. Cool and slice to serve. You can also place it in a freezer to serve later.

Soup and Stews Recipes

21. Zürich-Style Stew

Preparation Time: 15 minutes

Cooking Time: 50 minutes

Servings: 4

Ingredients:

500 g natural seitan,

2 small onions, flour

1 dl white wine

1 dl soy cream,

2 tbsp. Extra virgin olive oil, salt, and pepper

Directions:

1. Cut the seitan into thin slices and flour them. Put the oil in a pan and brown the cleaned and thinly sliced onions, add the seitan and brown it quickly over high heat, stirring with a wooden spoon.
2. When the seitan begins to brown, add the wine, salt, and pepper and continue cooking for a few minutes.

Bind with the cream and finally serve with a side dish of rosti, potatoes boiled in their skins the day before, then grated or cut into very thin slices and then browned in oil, turning several times.

3. When they are browned, pick them up to form a pie, which is cooked again until a golden, crispy crust has formed.

22. White Stew

Preparation Time: 15 minutes

Cooking Time: 50 minutes

Servings: 4

Ingredients:

500 g seitan cut into pieces,

4 carrots cut into large pieces,

2 onions finely chopped

a celery stalk cut into small pieces,

2 tbsp rosemary,

A tbsp of extra virgin olive oil,

A tsp of shoyu,

2 cups of water,

a tsp of kuzu dissolved in a cup of cold water

Directions:

1. Sauté the onions in a little oil until they become translucent, then the rosemary for a couple of minutes, the carrots for a minute, the celery for another minute, and finally sauté everything for another 10 minutes.
2. Add water and cook for 5 minutes, then add the seitan and cook everything for fifteen minutes. At the end of cooking add the kuzu, allow to thicken, and turn off.

23. Stew with Potatoes and Vegetable Ragout

Preparation Time: 15 minutes

Cooking Time: 50 minutes

Servings: 4

Ingredients:

__For the Stew:__

400 gr of grilled seitan,

250 g of tomatoes,

150 g of potatoes,

Shallot,

Extra virgin olive oil,

Tarragon,

Salt

__For the Meat Sauce:__

100 gr of mushrooms champignon,

100 gr of peas,

100 gr of leeks,

Salt

Directions:

1. Cut the seitan into small pieces; blanch the tomatoes, remove their skin and dice them. Slice the shallot and brown it in a pan with a little oil. Add the diced potatoes.
2. Place the shallots and potatoes in an oven dish greased with oil; bake at 180°F for 30 minutes. After this time, add the seitan and cook for another 10 minutes. Remove the dish from the oven, add tomatoes and tarragon, and mix.
3. Separately, in a saucepan, heat the sliced mushrooms and leeks in a little oil, add the peas, a dash of water, and salt; braise for 10 minutes. Arrange the seitan in the center of a plate and surround it with the vegetable ragout.

Dinner Recipes

24. Seitan Zoodle Bowl

Preparation Time: 15 minutes

Cooking Time: 20 minutes

Servings: 4

Ingredients:

5 garlic cloves, minced,

Divided ¼ tsp pureed onion

Salt and ground black pepper to taste

2 ½ lb. Seitan, cut into strips

2 tbsp avocado oil

3 large eggs, lightly beaten

¼ cup vegetable broth

2 tbsp coconut aminos

1 tbsp white vinegar

½ cup freshly chopped scallions

1 tsp red chili flakes

4 medium zucchinis, spiralized

½ cup toasted pine nuts, for topping

Directions:

1. In a medium bowl, combine half of the pureed garlic, onion, salt, and black pepper. Add the seitan and mix well.
2. Heat the avocado oil in a large, deep skillet over medium heat and add the seitan. Cook for 8 minutes. Transfer to a plate.
3. Pour the eggs into the pan and scramble for 1 minute. Spoon the eggs to the side of the seitan and set them aside.
4. Reduce the heat to low and in a medium bowl, mix the vegetable broth, coconut aminos, vinegar, scallions, remaining garlic, and red chili flakes. Mix well and simmer for 3 minutes.
5. Stir in the seitan, zucchini, and eggs. Cook for 1 minute and turn the heat off. Adjust the taste with salt and black pepper. Spoon the zucchini food into serving plates, top with the pine nuts and serve warm.

25. Tofu-Seitan Casserole

Preparation Time: 10minutes

Cooking Time: 20minutes

Servings: 4

Ingredients:

1 tofu, shredded

7 oz seitan, chopped

8 oz dairy-free cream cheese (vegan)

1 tbsp Dijon mustard

1 tbsp plain vinegar

10 oz shredded cheddar cheese Salt and ground black pepper to taste

Directions:

1. Preheat the oven to 350 F and grease a baking dish with cooking spray. Set aside.
2. Spread the tofu and seitan in the bottom of the dish. In a small bowl, mix the cashew cream, Dijon mustard, vinegar, and two-thirds of the cheddar cheese. Spread the mixture on top of the tofu and seitan, season with salt and black pepper, and cover with the remaining cheese.
3. Bake in the oven for 15 to 20 minutes or until the cheese melts and is golden brown. Remove the dish and serve with steamed collards.

26. Seitan Meatza with Kale

Preparation Time: 10minutes

Cooking Time: 22minutes

Servings: 4

Ingredients:

1 lb. ground seitan

Salt and black pepper to taste

2 cups powdered Parmesan cheese

¼ tsp onion powder

¼ tsp garlic powder

½ cup unsweetened tomato sauce

1 tsp white vinegar

½ tsp liquid smoke

¼ cup baby kale, chopped roughly

1 cup mozzarella cheese

Directions:

1. Preheat the oven to 400 F and line a medium pizza pan with parchment paper and grease with cooking spray. Set aside.
2. In a medium bowl, combine the seitan, salt, black pepper, and parmesan cheese. Spread the mixture on the pizza pan

to fit the shape of the pan. Bake in the oven for 15 minutes or until the meat cooks.

3. Meanwhile in a medium bowl, mix the onion powder, garlic powder, tomato sauce, vinegar, and liquid smoke. Remove the meat crust from the oven and spread the tomato mixture on top. Add the kale and sprinkle with the mozzarella cheese.
4. Bake in the oven for 7 minutes or until the cheese melts. Take out from the oven, slice, and serve warm.

27. Roast Seitan

Preparation Time: 15 minutes

Cooking Time: 50 minutes

Servings: 4

Ingredients:

400 g natural seitan,

A sprig of rosemary

2 tbsp extra virgin olive oil

A clove of garlic,

A splash of tamari,

Salt

Directions:

1. Take the seitan and cut it into thin slices, mince the garlic and rosemary, place them on top of the slices, season with salt, and roll up as you would a normal meat roll.
2. Put it in the meat net, put it in an oven dish, add a drizzle of oil, the tamari, a pinch of salt, and two sprigs of the whole rosemary.
3. Fry it for 15-20 minutes. When cooled, cut into slices, and serve as desired accompanied by various vegetables.

28. Onions with Seitan

Preparation Time: 15 minutes

Cooking Time: 50 minutes

Servings: 4

Ingredients:

80 gr of seitan,

4 onions,

30 g of nutritional yeast,

A tbsp of chopped parsley,

3 tbsp of breadcrumbs,

2 tbsp Extra virgin olive oil,

Salt

Directions:

1. Peel the onions and cook them for 20 minutes in boiling salted water. Drain them, cut them in half, and hollow them out in the center to obtain small cups.
2. Put the yeast, parsley, and coarsely chopped seitan in a bowl and mix well. In a pan, brown the pulp obtained from the onions with a tbsp of oil. Cook it for 8-10

minutes with the breadcrumbs. Add salt and salt to the seitan mixture.

3. Fill the onions with this mixture, place them in an oven dish greased with oil, and bake in a hot oven at 200°F for about 30 minutes. Serve warm.

29. Lemon Escalopes

Preparation Time: 15 minutes

Cooking Time: 20 minutes

Servings: 4

Ingredients:

500 g seitan,

The juice of one lemon,

Flour,

Extra virgin olive oil,

Non-hydrogenated margarine,

2 tbsp salt, pepper

Directions:

1. Cut the seitan into slices and then dip in a layer of flour. Put two tbsp of oil in a large frying pan, place the seitan slices in the dressing and brown them on both sides over high heat.
2. Season with salt and pepper and cook for a few minutes. Remove them from the pan and arrange them on a serving plate, which should be kept warm.
3. Pour the lemon juice into the cooking liquid, add a knob of margarine mixed with a tsp of flour, and, stirring constantly, thicken the sauce. Pour it over the escalopes and serve immediately.

30. Seitan with Green Pepper

Preparation Time: 15 minutes

Cooking Time: 20 minutes

Servings: 4

Ingredients:

4 slices of seitan,

8 tbsp of green pepper,

1 tbsp of extra virgin olive oil

2 tbsp of white wine

2 tbsp one tbsp cognac,

1 dl soy cream,

Salt

Directions:

1. Crush the green pepper coarsely or drain it from the preserving liquid. Top the slices with it, pressing lightly so that the pepper adheres to the seitan.
2. Place a serving dish or 4 serving plates in preheated 180-degree oven. Pour the oil into a frying pan, heat it and brown the slices for a few minutes on both sides over high heat.

3. Add salt only when they are cooked and place them on plates heated in the oven. With a wooden spatula scrape the bottom of the pan, add the cognac and white wine, turn up the heat and allow it to evaporate.
4. When the bottom is reduced and thickened, add the cream and cook for a few more minutes, until you have a creamy sauce. Pour it over the slices and serve immediately.

Special Occasion Recipes

31. Basic Simmered Seitan

Preparation Time: 15 minutes

Cooking Time: 20 minutes

Servings: 4

Ingredients:

1¾ cups wheat gluten flour (vital wheat gluten)

½ tsp salt

½ tsp onion powder

¼ tsp sweet paprika

1 tbsp olive oil

3 tbsp soy sauce

1 ⅔ cups cold water

Simmering Liquid

2 quarts water

½ cup soy sauce

2 garlic cloves, crushed

Directions:

1. Make the seitan: In a food processor, combine the wheat gluten flour, nutritional yeast, salt, onion powder, and paprika. Pulse to blend. Add the oil, soy sauce, and water and process for a minute to form a dough.
2. Turn the mixture out onto a lightly floured work surface and knead until smooth and elastic, about 2 minutes.
3. Make the simmering liquid: In a large saucepan, combine the water, soy sauce, and garlic.
4. Divide the seitan dough into 4 equal pieces and place in the simmering liquid. Bring just to a boil over medium-high heat, then reduce heat to medium-low, cover, and simmer gently, turning occasionally, for 1 hour.
5. Turn off the heat and allow the seitan to cool in the liquid. Once cool, the seitan can be used in recipes or refrigerated in the liquid in a tightly sealed container for up to a week or frozen for up to 3 months.

32. Stuffed Baked Seitan Roast

Preparation Time: 15 minutes

Cooking Time: 20 minutes

Servings: 4

Ingredients:

1 recipe Basic Simmered Seitan, uncooked

1 tbsp olive oil

1 small yellow onion, minced

1 celery rib, minced

½ tsp dried thyme

½ tsp dried sage

½ cup water, or more if needed

Salt and freshly ground black pepper

4 cups fresh bread cubes

¼ cup minced fresh parsley

Directions:

1. Place the raw seitan on a lightly floured work surface and stretch it out with lightly floured hands until it is flat and about ½-inch thick. Place the flattened seitan between two sheets of plastic wrap or parchment paper.

2. Use a rolling pin to flatten it as much as you can (it will be elastic and resistant). Top with a baking sheet weighed down with a gallon of water or canned goods and let it rest while you make the stuffing.
3. In a large skillet, heat the oil over medium heat. Add the onion and celery. Cover and cook until soft, 10 minutes. Stir in the thyme, sage, water, and salt and pepper to taste. Remove from heat and set aside.
4. Place the bread and parsley in a large mixing bowl. Add the onion mixture and blend well, adding a little more water if the stuffing is too dry. Taste, adjusting seasonings if necessary. if necessary. Set aside.
5. Preheat the oven to 350°F. Lightly oil a 9 x 13-inch baking pan and set aside. Roll out the flattened seitan with a rolling pin until it is about ¼-inch thick.
6. Spread the stuffing across the surface of the seitan and roll it up carefully and evenly. Place the roast seam side down in the prepared baking pan. Rub a little oil on the top and sides of the roast and bake, covered for 45 minutes, then uncover and bake until firm and glossy brown, about 15 minutes longer.
7. Remove from the oven and set aside for 10 minutes before slicing. Use a serrated knife to cut it into 1/2-inch slices.

Note: For easiest slicing, make the roast ahead and cool completely before slicing. Slice all or part of the roast and then reheat in the oven, tightly covered, for 15 to 20 minutes, before serving.

33. Seitan Pot Roast

Preparation Time: 15 minutes

Cooking Time: 20 minutes

Servings: 4

Ingredients:

1 recipe Basic Simmered Seitan

2 tbsp olive oil

3 to 4 medium shallots, halved lengthwise

1 lb. Yukon Gold potatoes, peeled and cut into 2-inch chunks

½ tsp dried savory

¼ tsp ground sage

Salt and freshly ground black pepper

Horseradish, to serve

Directions:

1. Follow the directions for making Basic Simmered Seitan, but divide the seitan dough into 2 pieces instead of 4 before simmering. After the seitan has cooled in its broth for 30 minutes, remove it from the saucepan and set aside.
2. Reserve the cooking liquid, discarding any solids. Reserve 1 piece of the seitan (about 1 lb.) for future use by placing it in a bowl and covering it with some of the reserved

cooking liquid. Cover and refrigerate until needed. If not using within 3 days, cool the seitan completely, wrap tightly, and freeze.

3. In a large saucepan, heat 1 tbsp of the oil over medium heat. Add the shallots and carrots. Cover and cook for 5 minutes. Add the potatoes, thyme, savory, sage, and salt and pepper to taste. Add 1½ cups of reserved cooking liquid and bring to a boil. Reduce heat to low and cook, covered, for 20 minutes.
4. Rub the reserved seitan with the remaining 1 tablespoon oil and the paprika. Place the seitan on top of the simmering vegetables.
5. Cover and continue cooking until the vegetables are tender, about 20 minutes more. Cut the seitan into thin slices and arrange on a large serving platter surrounded by the cooked vegetables. Serve immediately, with horseradish on the side.

34. Seitan Sausage Jambalaya

Preparation Time: 10 minutes

Cooking Time: 40 minutes

Servings: 3

Ingredients:

2 tbsp vegetable oil

2 links Apple-Sage Andouille Sausage or Tofurky Andouille sausage links, cut diagonally into ⅓-inch slices

2 celery stalks, finely diced

1 green bell pepper, finely diced

1 small yellow onion, finely diced

2 garlic cloves, minced

5 scallions, green and white parts, diced

2 cups long-grain white rice

1 (28-ounce) can diced tomatoes, with juice

3 ½ cups vegetable broth

¼ tsp dried thyme

¼ tsp salt, plus more as needed

Black pepper

Directions:

1. In a large nonstick skillet over medium-high heat, heat 1 tbsp of the oil. Sauté the sausage for 5 to 7 minutes, until nicely browned. Transfer to a plate.
2. In the same skillet over medium-high heat, heat the remaining 1 tbsp of oil. Sauté the celery, bell pepper, onion, garlic, and three-quarters of the scallions for 7 to 10 minutes, stirring occasionally, until vegetables are tender.
3. Stir in the rice, tomatoes, broth, sausage, thyme, salt, and pepper to taste. Bring to a boil.
4. Reduce the heat to medium-low, cover the skillet, and simmer for 20 to 25 minutes, until the rice is tender, and all the broth is absorbed. Remove from the heat and let rest for 10 minutes, covered. Fluff the rice with a fork.

Taste and season with more salt and pepper, as needed. Serve garnished with the remaining scallions.

35. Fusilli with Seitan Ragout

Preparation Time: 10 minutes

Cooking Time: 40 minutes

Servings: 3

Ingredients:

350 gr of fusilli

250 gr of seitan

A rib of celery

Half carrot

Half onion

Some dried mushrooms

Little tomato sauce

Oregano

Extra virgin olive oil

Directions:

1. Chop celery, carrot, and onion and heat in a pan with a tbsp of oil. Soak the mushrooms in a little water.
2. Chop the seitan and add it to the herbs, then add the mushrooms, a few tbsp of tomato sauce, and cook for about 20 minutes.
3. Add the oregano and season the pasta with the sauce thus obtained.

36. Barbecue Tofu Burgers

Preparation Time: 10 minutes

Cooking Time: 30 minutes

Servings: 4

Ingredients:

14 ounces extra-firm tofu, drained and pressed

¼ tsp ground black pepper

½ tsp onion powder

½ tsp garlic powder

¼ cup barbecue sauce

2 tbsp ketchup

¼ cup chickpea flour

Directions:

1. Press and drain the tofu and crumble tofu into a large bowl. Mix tofu with the remaining ingredients.
2. Form mixture into 6 equal-sized patties.
3. Heat 2 tbsp olive oil in a large skillet, cook patties until browned on both sides.

Sides Recipes

37. Colorful Seitan - Rice Salad with Lamb's Lettuce

Preparation Time: 10 minutes

Cooking Time: 40 minutes

Servings: 3

Ingredients:

__**For the Rice:**__

2 cups rice

1 tbsp vegetable broth

4 cups water

__**For the Salad:**__

200 g seitan

2 red peppers

½ stick leek

3 small carrots

1 tbsp coconut oil some freshly ground

Pepper salt or vegetable broth for seasoning

Directions:

1. Cook the rice in the vegetable broth until not too soft, use wild rice if necessary.
2. While cooking, dice seitan, leek, bell pepper, and carrots.
3. Heat coconut oil and fry seitan, add carrot cubes, and fry until hot.
4. Put the cooked rice in a bowl with leek and bell pepper. Add braised seitan and carrot pieces, mix and season with spices.
5. Let it stand for half an hour. While this is happening, wash lamb's lettuce and spin dry.
6. Serve together with well-done rice salad to taste. The coconut oil enhances the taste.

38. Oriental Fruit-Vegetable Pilaf

Preparation Time: 10 minutes

Cooking Time: 40 minutes

Servings: 3

Ingredients:

For the Pilaf:

200 g rice salt

2 onions

1 clove garlic

50 g dried apricots

50 g raisins

50 g dates

200 g seitan

1 bunch of parsley

5 tbsp olive oil

50 g almond slivers

450 ml vegetable broth

2 tbsp tomato paste

1 tbsp honey 4 pointed peppers

400 g natural yogurt

1 bunch spring onions

For the Spice Mix:

1.5 tsp. paprika noble sweet

1.5 tsp. ground coriander

1.5 tsp. ground cumin

0.5 tsp. chili flakes

1 tsp. cinnamon

2 tsp Ras el-Hanout

Directions:

1. Cook the rice with 400 ml salted water in 10 min with lid on medium heat until not fully cooked. Meanwhile, finely dice the garlic, onions, and dried fruit. Dice the seitan and chop the parsley. Mix spice mixture well with all spices.
2. Heat 3 tbsp of oil in a high skillet. Sauté onions, garlic, and seitan a little. Add tomato paste, almonds, and spice mixture and sauté briefly. Deglaze with vegetable broth and stir in honey.
3. Fold in rice and let it absorb enough liquid for about 10 - 15 min at low heat.
4. Meanwhile, wash and remove seeds from pointed peppers, cut into quarters and sauté in a grill pan on both sides over medium heat until soft and browned. Mix the yogurt with half of the parsley and the salt, add additional seasoning to the dip according to taste.

5. Cut the spring onions into rings and add to the rice. Turn up the heat and roast the rice for about 5 minutes. Remove crust from pan several times with spatula until rice is browned.
6. Serve pilaf with paprika and dip.

Gravies, Sauces, And Glazes

39. Marinade Sauce

Preparation Time: 10 minutes

Cooking Time: 40 minutes

Servings: 3

Ingredients:

¼ cup soy sauce or Bragg Liquid Aminos

1 Tbsp liquid hickory smoke

¼ cup red wine

3 Tbsp white vinegar

½ tsp dry mustard

2 Tbsp dark or blackstrap molasses

1 tsp dill weed

¼ tsp pepper

¼ tsp cayenne

Directions:

1. Mix well or shake in a jar.
2. This sauce can be thickened with a tbsp of cornstarch and cooked until thickened and used over veggies, rice, etc.

40. Seitan Salami Jerky

Preparation Time: 10 minutes

Cooking Time: 40 minutes

Servings: 3

Ingredients:

In a greased casserole dish, layer the following in the order given:

2 cups sauerkraut

2 cups cooked barley (or other grains – I used a mix of barley, flaxseeds, and spelt as I had just a little of each left)

2 cups canned or cooked (rinsed and drained) beans (I used kidney, but any would work)

A little diced or ground seitan or salami

1 tbsp Breadcrumbs, nutritional yeast (sprinkle a little over the top)

1 tbsp Salt, pepper, other seasonings to taste

Directions:

1. Drizzle a little catsup over the top in an attractive pattern (other sauces would work, too, such as BBQ or spaghetti sauces. I only had catsup left)
2. Bake at 325F for 30 minutes. The kraut juice should keep this from sticking but add a little water if it seems too dry.

Options: Onion, garlic, or other veggies – add whatever you have that sounds good. We are in emergency survival mode here!

Conclusion

Congratulations on making it this far. Seitan is a vegan meat substitute based on vital wheat gluten flour, mixed with liquid to obtain a dough which is then cooked. Depending on the liquids and seasonings you use and how it's cooked, seitan can be made to look like beef, poultry, veal, salami, burgers, and more. Ready-made seitan can be purchased at some health food stores, but it's tastier, cheaper, and more fun to make your own.

Some vegans understandably don't like to compare anything to meat, but let's face it, many vegan converts still want that something on their plate that "looks" like meat. The history of seitan is vague, but it dates back centuries and is widely used in many Asian cultures.

CPSIA information can be obtained
at www.ICGtesting.com
Printed in the USA
BVHW040040050621
608823BV00013B/3900

9 781802 894585